CW00468421

LOVING HER

loving her

10 Loving Standards
to Call Forward the
Wealthy Woman
Inside You

REBECCA WIENER MCGREGOR

Printed in the United States of America

Cover and Interior design by Ally Vogel

Library of Congress Cataloging-in-Publication Data has been applied for.

ISBN   979-8-7698-3074-7

DEDICATION

*May this offering help you to uncover that part inside
of you that is both an endless spring of love and a fiery
flame of passion to fuel the ultimate act of self-love:
Creating and living a rich life that you love.*

CONTENTS

PART THREE: *living your rich life*

INTRODUCTION

As you read, I'd like you to know that I have intentionally left punctuation and grammatical errors, as well as typos in this book to show you that the message in your heart can come out imperfectly and still be extremely valuable.

It took a lot of effort for me to sit down and write this because I wanted it to be just right and valuable to you.

I am still working through my own gunk with perfectionism. I'm a recovering perfectionist, and I have danced with that for a long time. Being perfect is tied to my need to not be a bother or take too much space or cause problems for other people. And since you're going to take the time to read it, I want it to stir something in you that will shift you and make your life better, easier, simpler, and more fun.

Through my perceptions as a child, I learned to be a "good girl" by not causing any problems. I knew that there were plenty of other problems, disruptions, and I didn't want to add to them.

What I saw and heard was that if I was going to be good and helpful then I wouldn't be too loud, I wouldn't ask for too much, I wouldn't be naughty, I wouldn't rock the boat, I wouldn't cause a disruption.

And here I am still not wanting to cause any problems. No typos to make you think less of me or my thoughts.

Not writing this book at all meant that I wouldn't make any mistakes in my delivery which is why it took a year to get together, a couple of months to formulate, and only a couple of days to actually write.

The truth is that I really want to shake things up for you. I really want to disrupt the flow of old ideas and limiting beliefs that are actually hurting you, other women, and our society.

It has been many, many, many hundreds and thousands of years that women did not have any control of their money. In the U.S. it wasn't until the 1970's that women were allowed to open bank accounts and get credit cards without the permission of their husband or a male relative.

The truth is that it's normal and natural for you as a woman to wonder if you're good with money, to have blocks about money, to have limiting beliefs about money.

It's taken a lot for women to be able to be empowered about money and many still suffer in relationships—personal and professional—that are unkind, stifling, and downright abusive in the name of financial security.

I'm ready to bust through these old limits in order to save the lives of women living in abusive relationships and to help women create more wealth and impact in the world.

When women have wealth, according to studies like 2018 U.S. Trust Study of High Net Worth Philanthropy, they use it more often than men to create good in their families and communities through philanthropic pursuits. The study also mentions that one in four wealthy women will lively give to causes focused on women and girls, including women's health, violence against women, reproductive health, and girls' education and development. So you can see it's not just a bonus that we are loving empathetic beings, we will use our empathy to create good for our communities.

Let's create more opportunities to feel wealthy and abundant and to fearlessly express our passions to help ourselves and others make the world a better place.

My path to get here is deeply spiritual. I use the words God, Universe, Divine, and Source to mean facets of the same guiding force in my life. Please don't let that take anything away from your experience. Please insert whatever words you prefer to call your Higher Power. You always know what is true for you.

Please use the concepts I'm about to share to create a spark or fan the flame for creating a life that you love filled with rich experiences and wealth beyond your wildest imagination.

PART ONE

loving her

THE AWAKENING

$436. My stomach dropped. $436. That was everything.

We had just reached our vacation destination, and I thought I should actually check my bank account balance to see how much spending money I had in my checking account because I wasn't sure how much cash I had.

I didn't know anything. I was completely unaware and disconnected from my money.

I was running a 6-figure hypnosis and coaching practice with a waiting list, but I still didn't see her.

I had hundreds of successful clients, but I still didn't feel her.

I made plenty of money to cover my expenses and life, but I didn't connect with her.

I had ample opportunity to grow, but I didn't trust her.

I didn't know her, so how could I love her?

You might be wondering who I am talking about.

The Wealthy Woman inside of me.

Decades of my life were spent in some form of scarcity and lack.

From longing to find the love of my life and overgiving and overdoing in relationships to holding on too tightly to a false sense of security in my corporate job and later taking care of everyone else and trying to make things work financially for my clients, I never saw myself as someone who could be wealthy.

Don't get me wrong. I've dreamed of it. I've been an entrepreneur since a young age fantasizing about making money to buy the house of my dreams and having gorgeous luxury cars and handbags.

But I wasn't connected to wealth.

I was like a kid making her Christmas list.

I was like a kid WAITING FOR SOMEONE ELSE to deliver my desires to me.

What I learned that meant is that I didn't think I could create it myself.

It meant that someone else would have to bring it to me. Save me. Maybe even that fairytale prince to ride in to save me on his trusty steed.

Even as I write this, I feel so much love for the lost and alone part of myself that didn't know enough to believe in herself.

She was so caught up in passively longing for her desires and perpetuating a story of how she needed saving.

It never occurred to me that I could get all that stuff from the Christmas catalog myself and have the money to pay for it.

The best part was realizing that I didn't need all that stuff to prove that I was loved or that I was enough.

The stuff became less important. I still enjoy material things, but my relationship with them is very different now. I focus on what really matters to me now—love, trust, connection, fun, spirituality, personal growth, helping others heal and change the world with their gifts, and making a positive ripple in the world one moment at a time.

I feel wealthier now than at any other time in my life. My life is full and rich. I am grateful every day for the journey I am on.

A WEALTHY WOMAN
LIVING A RICH LIFE

Wealth and being a Wealthy Woman is about the money in your bank accounts and investments, the freedom to choose the path of how you earn your money, and it's about abundance in all forms in your life.

Wealth and abundance show up in our lives everywhere:

A deep well of faith and trust in yourself.
A group of quality, trustworthy, and loyal friends.
A lot of joy and pleasure in your life.
A deep spiritual connection and relationship with yourself.
A connection to your higher power.
Good health and a strong body.
Loads of fun and laughter.
A partner that respects and supports your vision and purpose.
A partner who you respect and support in return.
A passion and appreciation for life and its gifts.
An appreciation and a passion for knowledge.
An appreciation for your resources.
Knowing your passion and sharing your gifts while being well-paid and having fun.

As you can see, wealth is about money, and it's about so much more than money. It's about supporting yourself to create a life of deep joy, confidence, love, connection, trust, and prosperity in all forms.

reflections

*What does wealth and being
a Wealthy Woman mean to you?*

What does living a rich life mean to you?

FROM GOOD GIRL
TO WEALTHY WOMAN

Trying to be the good girl so someone would find me worthy enough to save meant that I held loads of limiting beliefs that I had to buy into that made me "good."

Maybe if I was good enough. Maybe if I was a really good girl then what I wanted would show up for me.

A cycle of good girl or even perfectionist thinking can tear apart worthiness and it can create an avalanche of limiting beliefs. Here are some examples:

If I was a really good girl

If I asked for permission

If I didn't hurt anyone

If I didn't cause any disruption

If I didn't ask for too much

If I was really grateful

If I didn't rock the boat

If I wasn't too loud

If I helped everybody

If I didn't ask for too much for myself

If I didn't seem weak

If I didn't argue

If I didn't have different opinions

If I didn't show off

If I didn't brag about my accomplishments

If I was overly grateful for everything

If I gave away my services

If I discounted the prices of my services for those who needed it

If I worked outside my regular schedule because it worked better for my client

If I answered all their phone calls

If I wasn't demanding

If I didn't push too hard or when I wanted

If I didn't confront anyone for betraying me

If I pretended I couldn't see what was really happening

If I just let things go without speaking up

If I was a cool girl

If I was the chill girl

If I was to the go-with-the-flow girl

If I wasn't too high maintenance

If I didn't take too long to do my hair

If I didn't wear too much makeup

If I just did my job

If I just made dinner

If I just paid for everything

If I just said okay

If I just said yes

If I didn't act differently

If I didn't get sick

If I didn't bother anybody

If I didn't ask for too much help

If I didn't ask anyone for any favors

If I over gave

If I over gifted

If I did everything perfectly

If I gave when I had no money

If I didn't take anything for myself

If I just took care of everybody else

If I was smart but not too smart

If I didn't interrupt

If I didn't ask for seconds

If I didn't ask for honesty

If I didn't ask for monogamy

If I didn't ask for loyalty

If I didn't expect too much

If I didn't negotiate my salary

If I didn't ask for a raise

If I didn't ask to be treated respectfully by my coworkers

If I never tattled

If I never fought for what was right

If I never begged for help

If I felt just enough guilt or shame to keep me quiet

If I was the martyr

If I never invested in myself

If I never asked anyone else to invest in themselves

If I never asked anyone to step forward

If I never corrected anyone

If I wasn't too emotional

If I wasn't too happy

If I wasn't too successful

If I wasn't too rich

If I wasn't too shiny

If I wasn't too fancy

If I wasn't too casual

If I wasn't too sad

If I didn't show my grief

If I just got over it

If I just moved on

If I just sucked it up

If I just walked it off

If I just keep it to myself

If I just play along...

You can see how quickly these kinds of thoughts can cycle out of control. Maybe for you the thoughts come from a fear about being the Bad Girl, the Dumb Girl, the Fat Girl, the Weird Girl, or some other label you've given yourself that places any kind of limitation on your success or happniess. All of those labels are based on thoughts that can be shifted into something that serves you and your spirit in a more effective way.

We have sneaky little thoughts, like these, rolling around in our minds all the time. Sometimes 70,000 thoughts a day! They are learned from our families, cultures, society, schools, and everywhere there are people expressing themselves.
HINT: it's happening everywhere, all the time!

While we cannot control every single thought, we can learn to notice seemingly small limitations that we place on ourselves. It can feel like one or two of these thoughts aren't a problem, but they can create major blocks about our worthiness, value, and our life vision.

When you put them together they are a recipe for playing small, for letting someone else lead, for not taking responsibility for yourself, for not having to take any blame when things didn't work out, and for hiding from your greatness.

If you're doing one thing on this list, you probably don't feel too limited, but when these ideas are floating around and popping up, they are limiting you in ways you don't even realize. This list keeps us small, it keeps us under the control of our ego, and it keeps us from growing into who we can be.

As children, we learn these things by watching others, and they become our truths. This is actually normal and natural. We are little sponges picking up data and using it to adapt to the world without thinking if it is bringing us closer or further away from our goals. We don't start to care about what we are learning until much later in life when we start to actually care about goals, dreams, visions, and our purpose.

You may have felt sad or angry as you read this list. You may have seen yourself in the words or even between the lines.

It is okay.

Try not to judge yourself about it. Really, I mean it. Simply acknowledge the ones that you have picked up and maybe others that I haven't mentioned around motherhood, religion, your vocation.

Acknowledge them and breathe. You're not broken.

And at the same time let yourself be stirred up.

We don't know how out of balance things are until we take stock.

You get to realign and recalibrate with beliefs that actually support your goals, vision, desires, and passion.

Stand up right now. Shift your body. Take a breath.

Stand in your power and give yourself permission to go from good girl to Wealthy Woman.

reflections

*Reflect, Acknowledge,
Refrain from Judgment*

*What Good Girl beliefs are you
carrying around with you?*

*What beliefs do you believe keep
you from being a Wealthy Woman?*

*What did it feel like to give
yourself permission?*

Starting where you are.

As women and humans in general, we spend so much time trying not to rock the boat and accept everything that's given to us that we forget that we get to choose so much of our lives.

We get to choose what we think, what we believe, how we react and respond, and how we move forward. It's not so easy when we are out of practice or if we've never tried. But it gets easier and can even become automatic with practice.

I recognize that not everyone has the same starting place. Some of us have it easier than others because of our race, culture, religion, and current circumstances, while those very things have made it incredibly harder for others.

Dear Sister,

I see you. I have faith in you and the Divine Spark that lives in you. No matter where you are, do not lose sight of the vision that you hold for yourself. This journey to your vision that you have chosen might be the fight of your life. When you put your hand on your heart, feel it beating. Know that this journey chose you as much as you chose it.

You get to learn and grow and create a path for yourself. Fight for yourself if you must. Know that fighting for yourself is the most loving act because you will heal yourself, you will heal your ancestors, and you will heal your descendants in the process. No one loses when you fight for yourself.

You are worth every bit of effort it takes. You won't fight forever. Your awareness will shift, your habits will appear, and living and loving yourself on your journey will become automatic as you begin to lead yourself and your life in this new way.

I believe in you.

Love, *Rebecca*

START NOW

"Belief creates behaviors."
Neale Donald Walsch

When I decided that day on vacation that things had to change around my money, I realized that I had to change my beliefs because they were limiting me and my freedom.

Limiting beliefs are thoughts that we have learned to think over and over again that limit our success, happiness, possibility, joy, self-love, self-trust, and wealth.

Here's the path of limiting beliefs:

- You think thoughts over and over and they become beliefs and truth.
- Your beliefs define how you think.
- How you think influences how you behave.
- How you behave determines the circumstances in your life.
- The circumstances reinforce your beliefs.
- And we start all over again in a loop.

Here is an example of a path based on a very common limiting belief.

I don't have enough time.

I have so much to do.

I wish I had more time.

I wish that things would move faster.

Why am I always caught at this traffic light?

It takes me forever to get anywhere.

Why do I have all of these distractions?

It takes so long to get anything done.

I don't really want to do this, but I said I would be here so here I am.

Can you believe that took so long?

I didn't want to go in the first place.

I'll never get things done now.

Start a business? Are you kidding me!? I don't have enough time.

Take a class? You've got to be joking. When would I fit that in?

Have kids? I don't have time for myself. How would I do that?

You realize you have a limiting belief about time, so you start to change the way that you think.

Here's what happens:

I always have plenty of time to do what matters to me.

I have a lot to do, and I know when I focus my energy, I can complete it.

I am clear about my intention and vision.

I know exactly what I need to do, and I speak lovingly to myself to take action.

I know my schedule, and I give myself plenty of time to get where I need to go.

It's nice to take a pause at this stoplight.

I can drive with ease and arrive safely at my destination.

I am here because I chose to be.

I can be fully present in the moment.

I get to decide what to do next.

I am intentional about my life and my focus and that creates more time.

For someone who practices mindful awareness and notices what they are thinking these kinds of thoughts can become the default.

Notice the thoughts are easier and not rushed. They aren't causing anger or frustration. They are relaxed and in the present. They are energized by doing what is important to them.

Give yourself a breath. This is what is possible for you. If you're here sometimes, then you get to be here more often. If you're not quite here, you can get to this place with a bit of practice.

You can see when you shift your beliefs how much of an impact that makes on how you think and behave and what you create in your life.

Therefore, your life is a reflection of your beliefs and your state of being. The good news is that you get to shift your beliefs to create the kind of life that you want.

My desire for you is that you create a life of love and abundance in all areas of your life. You don't have to choose one area of your life over another. When you shift, everything else shifts with you. You are the common denominator of your life.

Here and now you get to shift. You get to see money and wealth in a whole new way. You can see it as something that is actually meant for you, too. You can see it as something that you can create for yourself without needing to rely on anyone else to come and save you.

Now does this mean that you don't ever rely on anyone and that you become an island? No, it does not mean that.

It means you don't have to stay somewhere that is unfulfilling or unsafe in the name of money. That's just fake financial security.

You have the power inside of you to create wealth all on your own. You don't need anyone else to believe that you can do it. You are *the only one* who has to believe it.

Right here and now can be that place, that time, that moment when you start to believe that you can create wealth and abundance in all forms (an abundance of love, trust, connection, fulfillment, energy, time, joy, and more) in your life.

Get used to this phrase and what it means for you:
I am creating wealth and abundance in all forms in my life.

Your first question is, "How?!"

How can I do this?

How is it possible for me to create wealth and abundance in all forms in my life?

The *how* will make itself known to you as you. As you shift your thinking; your feelings, actions, behaviors, and reactions will follow suit.

You absolutely 100% get to believe that this is possible for yourself. Even though you have never believed it before. You have witnessed other people with wealth and abundance around you, so you know that it is possible.

your vision

for your life is possible for you if:

You desire it.

It feels good and right and natural to you.

These are the only qualifiers.

You don't have to know how, only that
it gets to be possible for you.

Let things open up for you. Let yourself have fun!

PART TWO

wealthy woman standards

WEALTHY WOMAN STANDARDS

"The minute you settle for less than you deserve,
you get even less than you settled for."
Maureen Dowd

A standard is a way of being. It's a way of living. It's not a boundary that keeps you on guard. A standard sets you free. It becomes a matter of fact. It becomes a way to live your life with certainty and alignment. It is a belief that you can create as a personal truth that is based on your values.

Think of standards as Standard Operating Procedures for you as a Wealthy Woman. These are the ways that you are choosing to think and believe no matter what is going on around you. Rather than holding guard with a boundary, you get to operate from a place of "this is simply the way it is for me."

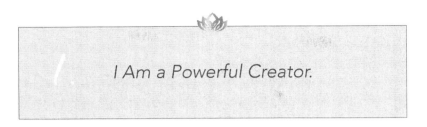

I Am a Powerful Creator.

Hand on heart. Feel the power of that statement in your body.
I Am a Powerful Creator.

You are a piece of the Divine, God, Source, and The Universe.
That's where you came from, so that is what you are.

To paraphrase one of my very favorite teachers, Dr. Wayne
Dyer, who liked to say that we must be like what we came from.
If you cut a pumpkin pie and take out a slice, the thing you take
away is still pumpkin pie. If you take a sample of blood from
your body, the assumption is that it must be like what it came
from, so you can test your cholesterol from any vein in your
body and the answer will be the same.

You must be like what you came from.

Therefore you are a piece of the Divine.

Even if you only believe it's a sliver of you that is Divine, you are
nonetheless.

You are creating when you are in a good mood, a sad mood,
when you are in your stories, in your limiting beliefs, in your
programs, in the flow of abundance. It is never not true.

This has many helpful consequences and opportunities.

This means that you get to treat your existence as a sacred experience.

You get to release yourself from the putdowns, judgments, and negative self-talk that has been running in your mind.

You get to practice treating yourself as the Divine being you are.

You wouldn't speak to the Divine or even your best friend the way you have sometimes spoken to yourself.

Right here, right now get up and look in the mirror.

See who you are beyond your body. Look into your own eyes and find the sparks of the Divine waiting there to connect with you. See the Divine looking back at you with wonder and amazement at your specialness, unique gifts, loving heart, and your passion and purpose. Feel the delight of loving and being loved just for existing.

You have nothing to prove. You are already perfect. You are already whole. You are already worthy. You are already deserving of your desires. Abundance is your birthright.

Your productivity doesn't define you.

Your knowledge doesn't define you.

Your body doesn't define you.

Your skills don't define you.

You get to step into these beliefs now.

When you accept this as a standard and a way of being, you release yourself from judgment. You take back all of the energy that was spent on figuring out how to prove to yourself and everyone else that you are enough. Instead, you get to use that energy to notice your feelings, emotions, and experiences and help yourself come back into alignment with your desires.

You have the power to create outcomes for yourself by what you decide to feel about your circumstances. You create your feelings, emotions, and experiences.

Whatever your background, religion, or name of your higher power you have been given an opportunity to co-create and create your life in every moment.

This is true all of the time, not just when you decide to manifest or attract something to yourself or achieve a goal. This is happening every minute of your life. You are either creating the same experience or forging a path for a new one.

The truth of this is a lot of responsibility and a lot of freedom.

As you are a piece of The Divine, then so is everyone else.

The freedom is that everyone else can do it, too.

Whether they want to acknowledge it or believe it or not, it is true for them, too.

This is where freedom comes in.

You no longer have to try to control or overgive or move obstacles for anyone.

You no longer have to save anyone.

You no longer have to try to create an outcome for anyone.

You no longer have to try to manifest anything for them.

When you decide that you have to take over and do for them, you are diminishing their power to create their reality.

You are expressing your lack of trust in them and their abilities.

They have the power, too.

This doesn't mean that you are off the hook for supporting, encouraging, loving, and so on, but it does allow you to see others as powerful beings themselves.

You no longer have to pull anyone up to your level because they are already here.

You no longer have to feel someone is higher or lower than you.

You get to release judgment about where everyone else is in their lives.

You still get to choose whether or not to be around them, work with them, love them, and not be responsible for their circumstances.

This is all-important because you have to take focused energy and responsibility for what you are creating for yourself.

You get to uncover and clarify your desires and behave in a way that expresses what you would like to create.

If you want to create a deeper love for yourself, you get to work on seeing yourself as loveable and worthy.

If you want to create a career for yourself, you get to cultivate trust in your gifts and your ability to use them to help yourself and others.

If you want to create an impact, you get to practice believing in yourself enough to be visible, so the people you want to help can find you.

You get to pour love into yourself with the understanding that your existence is sacred.

You get to feel deep devotion to who you are now, who you would like to become, and the spectacular journey to get there.

You get to pour love into your life with the understanding that each moment is a sacred experience.

You get to know and understand that you can be a perfectly imperfect human being and at the very same time you are Divine.

You get to feel your worthiness grow as you think of and care for yourself in this way.

You get to see others as worthy and amazing as well.

As you release judgment of yourself and others because you hold the standard that everyone has the Divine in them, it frees space in your mind. In that space, you get to allow inspiration, creativity, solutions, grand visions for your life, and an expansion of your imagination.

When the cloudiness of judging yourself and others dissolves, possibilities will open up beyond your imagination. You can avoid jealousy of what others have created for themselves because you have the power to create for yourself.

Instead of being jealous, congratulate them for showing you that creating your desires is possible!

As you practice this standard, notice your thoughts, emotions, words, and actions.

Try not to be in judgment of yourself, but rather practice noticing what you are thinking, feeling, how you are being, and what you are doing and ask yourself:

- Does this make sense based on my desires?
- If I were to think differently, what would it be?
- If I were to feel something else, what would it be?
- If I wanted to behave in another way, what would that look like?
- What would the outcome be using these alternatives?

Set intentions for what you'd like to create in your life each day, week, month, and so on.

Practice talking about your desires.

Avoid speaking about things you hate/dislike.

Avoid speaking gossip.

Instead of being jealous, congratulate them for showing you that creating your desires is possible!

I Am a Powerful Creator.

affirmations

Place your hand on your heart. Connect to yourself. Speak each of these statements out loud 30 times until you feel a shift in your body. Journal what happens in your body and mind. Repeat these often as you strengthen these beliefs in yourself. Trust in the power and vibration of your vocal cords. As you speak, you will feel the transformation begin.

I use my attention and intention to create the life that I love.

The ultimate act of self-love is to create a life that I love.

My life is a sacred experience.

I am devoted to my vision.

I claim and reclaim my power to create a fulfilling dream life.

I stay connected to my thoughts, feelings, and actions, and know that I can shift whenever I decide.

I celebrate my success and the success of others easily and automatically.

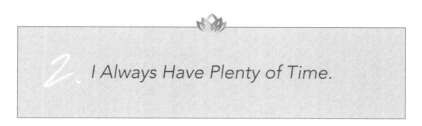

2. I Always Have Plenty of Time.

*"Time isn't precious at all, because it's an illusion.
What you perceive as precious is not time, but
the one point that is out of time: The Now.
That is precious indeed. The more you are focused
on time—past and future—the more you miss the
Now, the most precious thing there is."*
Eckhart Tolle

Time is often considered one of your most valuable assets. You spend time in ways that you can never recall. You have all sorts of ideas about how you have wasted time, spent it poorly, there not being enough time, and even wondering if you can fit in everything you want to do.

The lack or scarcity of time is also one of the most common limiting beliefs. When people talk about what they desire and are asked what is stopping them from having it, the most common answers are that they don't have enough time or money.

Since we all have the exact same amount of time each day. You get to create a new relationship with time. Relationships are give and take. You get to have a loving respectful relationship with time.

It's important to honor your relationship with time using it as wisely as you can. How you spend your time is the real indicator of what is possible.

If you spend your time procrastinating, you will never have enough.

If you spend your time longing for more time, you will never have enough.

If you spend your time avoiding the tasks that will drive your life forward, you will never have enough.

If you spend your time distracted by your past, you will never have enough.

If you spend your time worrying about the future, you will never have enough.

It is only when you bring yourself into the present moment as often as possible each day that you can actually expand time.

Believing that you always have enough time allows you to look at the time in a fresh new way. You get to interact with time, you get to enjoy the time, you get to notice how you slow down or speed up time based on how you are thinking and feeling in the present moment.

This is a gift that you have.

You have been in a situation in your life or the day before you got to see your loved one felt like three days. And you've also been at an event where you were having a blast and you were there for eight hours, and it felt like a blink.

Now imagine for a moment that you always have plenty of time.

When you trust that you always have enough time, what do your days look like?

How are you behaving?

What do you feel?

Do you notice that you are moving closer to or further away from your goals?

You can actually shift the way you feel about time and how it is progressing simply by shifting your focus, clarity, certainty, and intention.

The number one way to move time along toward your goal is to have absolute clarity about what it is that you desire.

When you know beyond a shadow of a doubt that there are no other options to distract you, you can move in the pursuit of the singular desire.

It will show up faster for you and easier than you ever thought possible because you are not distracted by all the other options.

The same is true with certainty. Clarity and certainty are powerful boosters to your navigational system. Knowing what you want and being insistent that there isn't another option that would be right for you, allow you to move quickly because you bypass distraction and confusion altogether.

When you move with certainty, you increase your self-trust. You begin to adjust for this desire to be happening right now. You begin to feel the way you want to feel in the future right now. This allows your desire to unfold even faster, and suddenly you are closer to your vision than you realize.

Another way to help you collapse time is to be in your intention and to be thinking about your desires with such a beautiful focus that you are taking an active role in creating them.

Three guiding questions are:

What do I want to create for myself?

Why do I want to create that?

Right now, am I moving closer to or further away from my vision?

Release the old habits of waiting for someone else to bring your desire to you, believing it's something that you can't create, losing focus on it, or deciding you don't have enough passion to give it the time it deserves. Choose to believe that you always have exactly the perfect amount of time and you get to choose what you do with it.

Trying to find balance.

Balance is a feeling. Balance is a relationship with your intention. Balance is not a time card or a scorecard. Balance is about allowing yourself to be fully present wherever you are so that you're not emotionally or mentally pulled somewhere else.

When you feel pulled to some other area of your life, it's easy to feel out of time.

When you are at work and feel like you should be with your family, you don't have enough time for family.

When you are with your family and feel like your work is incomplete, you don't have enough time to work.

When you practice being fully present in your current experience, you create more focus, you have an opportunity to create more intention, and this creates more space and time to complete your tasks.

If you need a little shift to get you into the present moment, ground yourself by looking at and appreciating the details of your surroundings. Notice the green things, the red things, the black things, and the yellow things. Notice how your heart is beating; notice how your body feels standing or sitting in your chair; notice the temperature, the sounds, and the scent of the moment.

Release yourself of all time guilt by being here now while operating from your intentions. It's true. You can't be everywhere at once. You don't need to be. Be here, focused, and passionate about right now, and when you move to your next thing, do the same.

A simple practice is to set an intention for the moment. An intention can be just a simple desired outcome for the moment, the hour, or the day. If you are at work, set a work intention. If you are taking care of yourself, set a self-care intention. When you are with your loved ones, set an intention there. It doesn't have to be a formal log-in and log-out process but rather a breath or two while reminding yourself what you want to create right now.

2 *I Always Have Plenty of Time.*

affirmations

I can collapse time with my focus, clarity, and intention.

The more certain I am, the faster I see my desires.

I honor my relationship with time by being present now.

I honor my relationships with my loved ones by being focused, actively listening, and engaging with them.

I honor my work vision by creating small goals each day and being present.

I allow time for work, play, and rest.

3. I Am Responsible for My Own Energy.

"The purpose of life is to be restored back to love moment to moment. To fulfill this purpose, the individual must acknowledge that he is 100 percent responsible for creating his life the way it is. He must come to see that it is his thoughts that create his life the way it is moment to moment. The problems are not people, places, and situations but rather the thoughts of them. He must come to appreciate that there is no such thing as "out there."

Ihaleakala Hew Len

You are an energetic being. Whatever you feel is constantly rippling out of you. No matter where you go or what you do, you take your energy and ripple with you. It affects you, and it affects everyone else.

Your energy is your introduction.

No matter how or where you meet someone, your energy has been giving them information before you even open your mouth.

Your energy is your mindset, your emotional state, and whether or not you are present in the moment. And it is felt before you say a word.

Think about that time you were talking to your friend, and you noticed she kind of checked out for a moment. Remember how you just knew she was distracted?

Think of how when you shake someone's hand, you can tell if they are present or not. Think of that moment when someone frantically shows up to the meeting a minute late and carries that big wave of frazzled energy with them. You can feel all of that, can't you?

Everyone else can feel your energy too, so it's essential to show up the way that you want to show up. It's important to do this in an authentic way, too, because you can certainly tell when someone is faking it. ***Do not try to fake your energy.*** You will feel like an imposter, and others can see right through it. Whether they notice it consciously or unconsciously, it will change how they respond to you.

Here's how to show up in great energy that is authentic for you. Practice this right now so that you know how to do it before your next introduction, date, client meeting, Zoom, phone call, interview, and even when you walk into your home to be with your family.

Tune in to your attitude.

Check your emotions.

Notice where your focus lies.

Pay attention to your posture and body language.

Note any tension in your body and release the holding places.

Take a breath.

When you want to shift into a better feeling state of being, think about some great memories of how you were a great leader, created something special, or something that you love. Remember Gratitude is the highest vibration you can feel, so you can't go wrong feeling authentically grateful.

Then bring yourself and those good feelings back to the present moment.
Keep breathing—gently and naturally.

Remember to find the energy that is authentic for you.
No faking it. You don't have to fake it. And you can't fake it.
If you try, you'll know it, and so will others. Allow yourself the moment or two to get into a great place.

You deserve to feel this good most of the time. I say most of the time because life is a perfectly imperfect and sometimes a downright messy experience. You get to feel all of it. You get to grow from all of it.

If you're finding that you're not showing up the way that you want to because you are feeling stuck, anxious, small, disempowered, or generally uncertain, it is your responsibility to heal, adjust, recalibrate, and shift.

Because you are responsible for your energy, you are also responsible for what memories, stories, and beliefs created or caused your energy. This doesn't mean that you are responsible for the actions of others toward you. It means that even though you cannot control what happened to you in the past, you are in charge of your healing.

You are in charge of handling your emotions, healing your emotional wounds, growing, and learning new ways of being that help you feel the best possible emotions and energy.

This is for you first and everyone else second.

You deserve to feel the power of healing.

You deserve to feel the power of forgiveness.

You deserve to feel the power of acceptance.

You deserve to feel the power of confidence.

You deserve to feel the power of self-trust.

You deserve to feel the power of self-worth.

You deserve to feel all of this and more rippling out of you.

And the people around you deserve to feel the best possible energy from you as well.

Does this mean you are perfect and never have a dip of energy, pain, struggle, fear, sadness, or anger? Of course not. But it does mean that you are in charge of managing the consequences of getting stuck in that energy as well as dealing with the consequences of those around you getting caught up in it.

From a pure integrity perspective, remember that what you feel other people can feel too. Whether or not they are tuning in to those feelings or not makes no difference. Everyone is dealing with their feelings, emotions, and energy, and they don't deserve to have to deal with yours too.

You can see that statements like "this is just how I am" or "I can't help the way that I feel" get to be released from your vocabulary. Subscribing to this idea that feelings or ways of being cannot change is a sure way to stay stuck in unhappy, unfulfilling patterns. But that's not why you are here.

You are a beautifully flexible, adaptable, resilient being. You get to trust in your body, mind, and spirit, and its ability to heal itself. You get to trust that there is a better way of feeling and rippling on the other side of the pain. You get to be the one who learns from pain and experiences the satisfaction of growth and transformation.

As you lead, it is imperative that you heal and manage your energy. Do not place it on the person you are leading to decipher, read between the lines, or fight to ignore your energy to get to your message. Whether you are leading your family, leading a team, or leading a movement, keeping your energy in top form and aligned with your message will help you make the desired impact.

I Am Responsible for My Own Energy.

3.

affirmations

I lead with my energy.

My energy is my introduction.

I know the value of my energetic ripple.

My energy is my ripple in the world.

I am the only one who can shift my energy.

I choose my energy when I choose my thoughts and actions.

I am powerful and so is my energy.

4. I Am Responsible for My Own Happiness and Success.

"If you look to others for fulfillment, you will never be fulfilled. If your happiness depends on money, you will never be happy with yourself. Be content with what you have; rejoice in the way things are. When you realize there is nothing lacking, the world belongs to you."

Lao Tzu

There is no knight in shining armor coming to save you from yourself. There is no magical spell that will flip the switch for you. No one can make you happy. They can add to or take away from your happiness momentarily if you allow it, but the foundation of happiness is your responsibility. It's your responsibility because you are the only one who can do it.

Daily spiritual, self-care, self-love practices, intentions, commitments to yourself and your desire builds and strengthens this foundation, so you can feel resilient and bounce back from difficult moments. This helps you to count on yourself for comfort and peace and not have to go looking outside yourself—a result that will not support you in the long term without taking a toll on someone else.

Expecting someone else to make you happy is a huge amount of responsibility to place on another person. Counting on them to do the work to make and keep you happy is an impossible expectation. For example, imagine choosing a romantic partner because they make you so happy and then burdening them with the task of making you happy, or worse, blaming them because you are unhappy. Sounds completely silly, doesn't it?

You can choose to see every circumstance in your life as neutral and how you choose to feel about it brings you anger, joy, sadness, ease, hope, gratitude, fear, or other emotion. As you choose how to feel about it, you will uncover beliefs and automatic judgments about how to feel or be in certain situations. The more you notice your thoughts and behaviors, the more clues you have about what your self-limiting beliefs are and experiences from your past that still need healing, forgiveness, and acceptance.

This is good news! It's a reminder that you have the power to change these things. The more you operate as a person who knows that when she needs love and healing, she can get that for herself, the more powerful, confident, and committed to your vision you will become.

The standards, *"I Am Responsible for My Energy"* and the *"I Am Responsible for My Own Happiness and Success,"* are the reasons that I hold a place in each day to practice gratitude, notice my successes, and practice forgiveness and acceptance of everything else.

I take time each day to write what I am grateful for, why I am grateful for it, and how it makes me feel inside. I do the same process with my successes. This helps me to connect with the feelings in my body and build awareness to all the ways that I get to feel happy and successful during my day.

Finding happiness and acceptance through forgiveness helps bring me back to my responsibility for how I feel and helps me reconnect to my intention for each day. Please note that I use these as a practice which means I do them imperfectly. I fall down. I miss a day or a week, and I get back into the habit.

You get to detach from suffering. You get to decide from wherever you are that things are different. You get to draw a line in the sand and decide here and now that things are different and better. That you are going to commit to yourself, your happiness, and success no matter what anyone says or thinks. And no matter what look they have on their face, the energy they are projecting, and or what they might say behind your back. None of it has anything to do with you.

People have said things behind your back that you never heard about, and it didn't change anything for you. Why would it change anything for you if you know about it? Your attachment to what others think is an ego response. Your ego is begging for someone to challenge you, to tell you that your ideas are terrible, or to doubt you out loud because your ego's job is to keep your perceived self safe. If your ego can keep you from changing, it has kept you safe. That's its job.

You don't have to worry about getting rid of your ego. You don't have to hate your ego. You don't have to be at odds with it. You do get to learn the vocabulary and tone of your ego so that you can differentiate it from your intuition, your Higher Self, and the Divine.

The vocabulary and tone of your ego will be fearful, angry, frustrated, panicked, unkind, mean, critical, judgmental, scared, childish, jealous, distracted, confused, and will want to sabotage your growth. You will quickly learn to recognize it.

Your intuition, your Higher Self, and the Divine will be loving, confident, creative, imaginative, certain, direct, assertive, and have great clarity.

You don't get extra points for suffering. Suffering won't get you anywhere faster. Suffering is like the sandbags weighing down the hot air balloon, and when you release the suffering, you float higher and begin to soar. You were not made for suffering. You were made for expansion and contraction, ups and downs, highs and lows. You are a pliable, adaptable, and resilient being.

Yes, there will be pain. Let that sink in. There will be pain. You are designed to feel pain, and you are designed to heal. You are designed to cry and to release the pain and energy through your tears. You are designed to let those feelings flow through you. Feeling pain in life is part of being human.

The trouble comes when you believe that feeling is the problem. Feeling pain, sadness, anger, jealousy, grief, and anxiety is not the problem. Judging yourself for feeling is the problem. Thinking that you are wrong or weak because you get hurt or upset is where the problems begin.

The painful experiences in your life are not here to stop you. They are here to show you what you can feel. They are here to show you that growth is possible. They are here to help you become the most alive version of yourself.

Somewhere along the way, you may have received a message that you should just be grateful for what you have, that you should use your tools and keep yourself from feeling, that you should not grieve the people who you have lost, that you should not have fear, that you should not be angry, that you should not get sad, that you shouldn't get any kind of negative feeling because that will mean you are evolved or something.

That message is false. That message is false. That message is false.

The path to happiness and success has a foundation in letting yourself be fully present to life as it happens with all the pain, pleasure, sadness, joy, and everything in between.

You are designed for expansion and contraction.

I used to feel ashamed for having down moments or bad days. As if they meant that I was doing something wrong in my life. I wanted to be the one who was always growing in the most positive ways and never messing up.

Remember, the recovering perfectionist thing? I would be really angry when I was in contraction. I would feel like I hadn't understood something that everyone else who was succeeding left and right already knew.

I have had off days and weeks before. A few years ago I was in the spins. That's what I call it. Nothing was working the way that I wanted it to. I went to the bedroom and gave myself a timeout. I breathed for what felt like an eternity (about 40 seconds). I thought about how I got here again. WTF went wrong with me that I was stuck in this crappy feeling? I breathed some more. As I lay there looking at the ceiling, I asked for guidance. I turned on YouTube and found a business video from a coach that I had been following.

As I watched the video, there were some tips being shared and I started thinking about how I can help people when they want to be helped, but I can't want them to heal more than they want it for themselves. It released a sense of responsibility for my clients' behaviors and even released me feeling yucky about whether or not they chose me to help them.

This is all really special and important to me because I had probably heard this information, but it didn't click for me until I was in my timeout.

I also realized at that moment that I would have never fully understood that idea and released that responsibility back to my client or potential client without that timeout.

I needed that "off day" to get frustrated enough to give myself a timeout and watch the video which inspired a bunch of internal shifts. I needed this contraction. I needed this moment to be quiet so that I could receive the message. And it wasn't long after, I had another huge breakthrough with my clients and my work which led me to have a huge income month. I mean like a month where my income was greater than my annual income from a couple of years before.

I realized that contraction and feeling that off day was an important part of my life. I released all the shame and embarrassment that I had been carrying about being imperfect and not in growth mode all the time like I assumed everyone else was having from their social media posts.

When you let yourself feel and have imperfect moments, you develop a deeper relationship with yourself. You can give yourself that space and love to have the moments and discover what the gift of that moment could be.

Not all of the moments and gifts are as obvious as that day, but they show up in those spaces that are open now that I've stopped judging every thought or feeling as bad or good. And the same will happen for you.

Truth be told, because of many of the things I've shared with you here, I don't have many bad days now. They have become fewer and farther between. I may have a rough moment or an hour and move forward. I say this not to brag but because I want you to know that it gets easier with practice.

I wasn't always like this. I spent a lot of my early adult life in victim mode blaming my boss that my job was terrible, crying to my mom that I couldn't stand it while not applying to any other jobs because I was afraid of losing money or losing security and great benefits. You can imagine with this mentality, I had many rough days.

I've spent the last 17 years healing myself by spending a significant amount of time with coaches and healers taking care of me so that I could be at my best for my life. And I've healed as I've helped my clients heal. I've tried to be my best client and practiced the techniques that I ask my clients to so that most days are pretty good. Yes, I am human, so I have moments during the day where I get irritated or frustrated or in fear, but it doesn't last as long because I've given myself space to feel.

When you feel an emotion that doesn't feel good, take a breath and just notice it, acknowledge it. Refrain from judging it or yourself for feeling it. Notice how it feels in your body. What part of you tightens or feels heavy? Let yourself cry or sigh or say the expletive that is sitting on your tongue. Keep letting yourself feel it.

Notice that the space in your head isn't as full as it used to be when you would get mad at yourself for feeling angry or upset, when you would wonder why you hadn't mastered the art of detachment, or when you thought you knew all the things so you shouldn't feel awful ever again.

As you are breathing and feeling, you are teaching yourself that it's okay to feel. The more permission you give yourself to feel whatever comes up, the less self-judgment there will be. The less self-judgment, the more space there is for loving yourself, for finding solutions when it's something you can solve, the more space there is for inspiration, and the more space there is for hearing the Divine speak to you and give you ideas for your next steps.

Your heart feels more open. Your chest feels lighter. Your head feels more peaceful. The feelings start to flow through you rather than getting stuck or trapped from all that self-judgment.

Imagine the emotion flowing out of your feet back into the earth to be recycled for good energy somewhere else.

And suddenly you're okay. Maybe not as great as you want to feel all the time, but better than you have been feeling. And you can look at what you're learning and how you're building this relationship with yourself where you listen to her and validate her emotions, and she doesn't have to scream to get your attention.

This partnership with yourself will be one of the most powerful alliances you can ever make because it allows you to give yourself exactly what you need at the moment you need it.

Here are several techniques and tools that I have used myself and with my clients to help you transform your relationship with your memories and emotions and help you heal your energy, and amplify your happiness.

Hypnosis

Emotional Freedom Technique

Ho'oponopono

Neuro Linguistic Programming

Breathwork

Meditation/Self-hypnosis

Reiki and energy healing

Spiritual Coaching

Counseling

Do your research and reach out if you want some guidance about what can work best for your situation.

4. I Am Responsible for My Own Happiness and Success.

affirmations

I take responsibility for my happiness and success.

In moments of doubt, fear, or sadness, I remember that I am adaptable, resilient, and designed to heal.

I can shift how I feel by shifting what I think.

I create space for myself to feel what needs to be felt without judgment.

I trust that happiness is meant for me too.

I allow myself to return to love and joy.

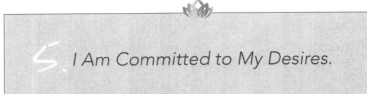

5. I Am Committed to My Desires.

*"You can have anything you want if you want it
desperately enough. You must want it with an inner
exuberance that erupts through the skin and joins
the energy that created the world."*

Sheila Graham

Living your life as a powerful creator and believing that your life
is a sacred experience, means that you get to take your desires
seriously because nothing with this much power behind it is an
accident.

You get to know and trust that your desires are placed in you
by the Divine. Whatever you have chosen to experience in this
life will come with desires and experiences for you to unfold.
All of your infinite choices are ready for you.

You no longer need to second guess your worthiness. You get
to choose your desires and breathe life into them. You choose
the whole process of discovering the path to your desires. You
choose to be open to receiving them, walking the path to meet
them, and even allowing them to be revealed to you.

Isn't this exciting? No more questioning why you have a desire.
No more questioning if you are good enough or worthy of your

desire. No more justification for your desires. You simply get to enjoy what comes into your imagination and decide which desires you bring to life. You are a powerful creator and you get to choose your path.

Having this incredible permission to release all of the old judgments or worries about what other people will think of you for having your desires can be a bit scary at first. Sometimes we get caught up in having so many options it can be hard to decide.

This is an opportunity for growth as well. This is an opportunity to tune in to what really really matters for you. This is an opportunity to notice when you stop yourself from your big desires, when you settle for something less, or when you walk away from a desire simply because it might be difficult to reach.

You were not made for small. You were not made for settling. You were not made for choosing your desires based on the easiest and shortest path. You were made for greatness.

The good news has two parts. First, you can do hard things. You can do things that take a lot of time and effort. You have reserves of strength you haven't even touched yet. You can create something out of nothing because you've done it in your life over and over and over.

Secondly, you can make hard things easier by peeling back all of the emotion and expectation attached to it. The things that you perceive as hard are only that way because of how you feel and believe about them and what you believe you have to sacrifice to get there.

Your desires are yours because of the person you will become on the path to achieving them. This is not a trick. This is not a happenstance. You honor and commit to your desires because of who you will become as you make them come alive.

As you bring your desires to form in your life, you are becoming the woman who can bring her desires to form. Read that again. You become more yourself with every step.

The more successes you have, the more you will trust yourself, and the greater the next vision or desire will be. You're a visionary. You have a glorious imagination. With each complete step, the next thing will keep showing up. Your next desire will make itself known to you.

More is what you're here for. More experiences. More love. More trust. More joy. More abundance. More growth. More days. More years. And you don't have to judge yourself a single bit for wanting more.

Your ego can and likely will flare up and decide that you are afraid, unworthy, or some other fearful idea because your desire may be huge or outrageous. In this case, it's likely that you will not know your next steps. That does not make you or the desire wrong or inappropriate.

Just take a pause and connect with yourself. When you are afraid, when you are suffering, or when you are in any experience of discomfort or questioning, ask yourself what you are learning. Ask yourself: Is this bringing me closer to or further away from my desires?

You will get an immediate answer and then lovingly decide what your next steps will be. If you need resources, find them.

If you need guidance, get it. If you need professional help, find it. You have access to infinite resources and infinite possible next steps. Just because you can't see them for a moment doesn't mean that they do not exist.

The other side of creating a desire or bringing it to form is to be open to receiving it in your life. As you are becoming the woman who can bring her desires to life, you get to create space in your life for your desires.

Work on creating space in your life to receive your desires. When in doubt do not choose the lesser things. Hold space and have patience for your true desire to come to you. Holding space and having patience do not mean stopping living or even waiting. It means allowing yourself to live while giving your desire space to arrive and doing so with deep faith and certainty that it will arrive.

Consider this: You have a space on your wall for a painting. You want an interesting piece of art for your space—something that you love and stirs you when you look at it.

You could easily go online and find something that looks nice with your room's color scheme and get something to fill that empty space. And that is a perfectly acceptable choice.

Or you can keep that space open until the painting that stirs you comes into your awareness. This is a small example of being committed to your desire rather than taking what is available.

This same scenario shows itself in other areas of your life as well. Entering into or staying in a relationship that is unsatisfying or even worse because the idea of the empty space was too much to bear.

The empty space is actually more loving than it is lonely. The empty space is there. The next step is to be open to receiving. Receiving is the other side of the loop of giving and gratitude. It's natural as a giving, loving, nurturing woman to not be comfortable with or connected to the idea of receiving.

Often women are caught up in giving and producing and pouring into others. Giving to their partner, giving to their children, giving to their friends, giving to their community, giving to their business, and carrying the mental load so the walls are up on their receiving. When I ask my clients if they are open to receiving, it's like a fresh idea. It was for me too.

The problem is that often in our giving, we feel like giving is our only choice. You may have an unconscious belief that things will fall apart if you stop, or you enjoy the benefit of being a martyr. If you're pouring into other people the focus is on them and not on you. Maybe giving is a safe space where you can hide from your desires or growth. When you get caught in giving or overgiving cycles, you can easily build resentment because you are not giving to yourself. This can be true even if you have been avoiding giving to yourself.

This resentment can build particularly if you believe that you feel that all of your efforts are not appreciated. This is dangerous territory. Resentment builds a cycle of anger that eventually erupts and causes guilt, shame, frustration, and a return to the output/doing because it feels safe and easy and well, it's what you know best.

You're not alone. This is a very human way of being. In this resentment, resistance, and frustration, you aren't connecting with your desires at all.

In order to receive, you must be willing to choose yourself. You must be willing to give to yourself.

Picture three large beautiful terracotta vases in a tray with a rim maybe 3-4" tall. When you look inside, the three beautiful vases are empty, bone dry, and maybe even have a cobweb or two. This is what happens when you are closed to receiving. When you don't give to yourself and when you don't allow others the pleasure of giving to you, your energy reserves are depleted.

Now imagine allowing others the joy of giving to you. They could be giving you a compliment, a tangible gift, help, support, encouragement, understanding, a listening ear, connecting you with something for your family, providing you with leads for your business, or even becoming a customer. You can feel the vases begin to fill.

Think about how it feels to give to yourself. Taking time to enjoy a walk, to think about what matters to you, spending time with your creativity, lighting your favorite candle and turning on music when you get into the bath rather than taking a quick shower, making sure that you always have on hand that brand of tea you love so much even though you have to special order it, praising yourself for good moments, and celebrating your successes. Notice how the terracotta vases are overflowing with love and energy.

The rimmed tray is now filling so rapidly and you feel loved, supported, and nourished.

Now imagine giving from the tray, from the overflow, rather than trying to extract the last droplets from the empty vases. It feels wildly different, doesn't it? Less resentment, frustration, anger, lack, or scarcity. More fullness, energy, joy, peacefulness, and grace.

When you are open to receiving and fully nourished, committing to your desires is easier because it's not just another thing on the to-do list. It's your life, it's your gift, it's your connection to the Divine and your Higher Self leading you to your next growth point.

Your desires—big and small—are yours for a purpose and you get to uncover and create your next level because of them. The more attention you give them, the clearer the vision, and the faster and easier the steps to getting there open up for you.

You can see now that choosing yourself does not mean that you don't care about others. It simply means that you must choose yourself—for your vision to become your reality. You must choose yourself to be your most fulfilled self for others. This is important to you because you are responsible for your happiness, success, and energy.

A simple practice to honor and care for your desires is to write them down when they come in. Think about them. Daydream about how the pieces look, feel, taste, smell, sound. Visualize them in completion in your meditation. Have fun with the idea that they are already here for you.

I work on my headspace with the tools I teach in my one-on-one programs and my Extraordinary Wealth course and community and those I've mentioned in previous standards. Hypnosis, Emotional Freedom Technique, Ho'oponopono, meditation, journaling, and several others in a specific way to clear the clutter in my head.

Why would you want to declutter your thoughts? Because when you have a lot of clouded, cluttered, and muddled thoughts, you get a traffic jam. When the traffic jam involves lots of thoughts of judgment, you shut out the opportunity to learn or to be inspired. You are less likely to notice opportunities happening right in front of you.

Here are some examples of judgmental thoughts:

Stories about myself and whether I am worthy of my desires.

Am I actually a good enough person for what I want?

Will I be able to handle the responsibilities of getting to my desires?

What if I mess everything up?

What if I have to let go of everything I have to get everything I want?

What if the prices for my desires are greater than I am willing to pay?

Acknowledging those thoughts and discovering the fear at the root helps me clear them and the corresponding feeling in my body. When I do this I create mental space for inspiration and for the steps to my desire to be shown to me. Inspiration is when you hear or feel the messages from the Divine, your Higher Self, God, Angels, and the Universe.

5. I Am Committed to My Desires.

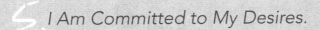

I can collapse time with my focus, clarity, and intention.

The more certain I am, the faster I see my desires.

I honor my relationship with time by being present now.

I honor my relationships with my loved ones by being focused, actively listening, and engaging with them.

I honor my work vision by creating small goals each day and being present.

I allow time for work, play, and rest.

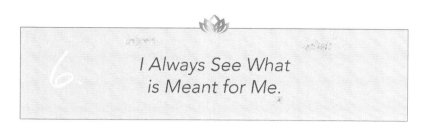

I Always See What is Meant for Me.

"There is no emergency. My divine timing is perfect and serves you well. Trust my sense of right action. Your successful unfolding is my great joy."
Julia Cameron

There are no missed opportunities. You never have to worry about someone else receiving something that is meant for you.

This is especially true in your work. For example, there are many coaches and hypnotists books that you could have in your hands right now, but my book is in your hands because I was meant to connect with you in some way.

For example, I do not have to worry that other people are writing books about being wealthy, creating abundance, loving yourself, or committing your desires. Because I wrote this one, I wrote it in my own special way with my own fingerprint and that is something only I can do.

This is also true for you. Whatever you create will be uniquely yours because you are not like anyone else and the experiences that led you to create it are not like anyone else's. You can know and trust that what is meant for will find you.

Another side of this beautiful standard is that what is meant for others will find them too. I'm talking about your children (Yes, you can still protect the children in your care by all means and still be open to this standard), your friends, your clients, and your neighbor down the street.

As a visionary, you will see obstacles in other people's paths long before they do. You'll see it as "she keeps dating that same personality in different bodies," or "she keeps overgiving to her clients and not charging enough to take care of herself," or "he doesn't feel smart enough for a great job," or "he keeps getting in trouble over and over even though I know he's meant for more."

Your initial response as a loving solution finder is to try to remove an obstacle for them. It doesn't work. The obstacle just moves it along in their journey. Instead of stopping to deal with it at Mile Marker 88, they will have to deal with it at Mile Marker 111 or somewhere further down the road.

The obstacle doesn't get resolved because you see it. It gets resolved when who it's meant for learns from it. We cannot learn for others. You can share your wisdom, lovingly guide them, and support them in their learning. And that is a loving act as well.

The fun part is that if you keep seeing obstacles for other people and you want to change things for them (and they haven't asked for your help or paid for your professional expertise) there is something for you to learn here.

It may come as a harsh lesson if you're not getting it. I've been there. I've had the big-wake-up-call-pain trying to help a friend who didn't really want it/wasn't really ready for it because she needed to learn her lesson.

I learned something powerful for myself about overgiving and overprotecting. I learned to dial back the advising and directing until it was requested. It felt cold at first. Because of my overgiving past, I didn't feel like a very good person not jumping in to rescue her. But it has gotten a lot easier and I learned that I get to save my energy for the myriad things I want to do in this world.

You can do it too. That includes moving yourself up on your priority list and learning your lessons, and being as loving and supportive as you can to those around you while you and they learn from life. Pouring into yourself when you feel the urge to pour into someone else will change your life.

No matter what you choose to do or the path you take, what is meant for you will find you. You cannot run from your desires. You cannot run from your lessons. You cannot run from what is meant for you. You can try. Yes. You can try with all your might to block these things from coming to you, to protect yourself from pain, to keep yourself from pleasure, and so on. It will still arrive for you. Whatever it is will take different forms until you allow yourself to see it.

It is all for you. Every bit of growth and experience that life has to offer you will always find you. You get to trust that whatever comes into your experience of life is for you.

You get to free yourself from the questioning of why or why not something has shown up for you. You get to move into a space of loving and trusting that you get to enjoy what is here now.

You get to release yourself from waiting. You get to move into a place of joyfully living and taking action knowing that what is meant for you will find you.

I hoped for a long time that I would get back together with a former partner. I was worried that he wouldn't find me if I moved and that if I started dating that I might actually fall in love or be so happy with the new person that I wouldn't be available when he came back for me. I stayed single. I avoided opportunities to meet people, and connect, and have fun.

And I suffered. Because I didn't trust that what was meant for me would actually find me, I had shut down my life. What found me instead of my former partner (thank goodness) was beautiful lessons about faith and trust in myself and my desires, discovering that I could ask for and receive the kind of relationship that I wanted rather than settling for what was boring, unbalanced, and unhealthy. What found me was my worthiness.

I would go through that relationship and what happened again because the lessons that showed up for me after it was all over changed my life in such a profound way. I have deep gratitude for who I was then. I honor her for doing the best that she could with the resources that she had. I appreciate her for allowing the lessons in when she did so that I could get back to my favorite thing—LIVING.

Trust yourself. Honor your experiences. Know that whatever is here is for you. And whatever you want will find you. If you want to live a rich life full of abundance, let it find you having fun, experiencing life, learning about yourself and others, discovering your creativity, deepening your spirituality, connecting with friends and loved ones, trying and failing, and being imperfect and messy. Let it find you truly living.

I Always See What is Meant for Me.

6.

affirmations

I trust in my vision for my life.

I trust myself to create with each step.

I trust myself to move forward in pursuit of my desires.

I enjoy living each day rather than waiting for things to happen.

I have faith in myself to notice every opportunity meant for me.

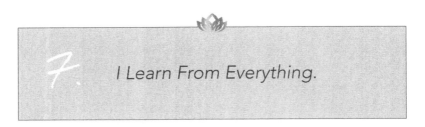

7. *I Learn From Everything.*

*"That is what learning is. You suddenly
understand something you've understood
all your life, but in a new way."*
Doris Lessing

There are no mistakes. Everything that is meant for you comes to you at some point. The experiences in your life are for you to enjoy and to learn from. It may be ugly and messy and painful and you can learn from it all.

"Everything happens for a reason" is overused and can be extremely hurtful when directed to someone else's painful circumstances. For example, I wouldn't say to someone who is grieving a death that everything happens for a reason. I would give them space to feel their feelings and support them as they feel the pain of loss and the uncertainty of how to move forward.

At the same time when we direct this idea to ourselves, it can be incredibly freeing because it releases us from the endless streams of questioning why something happened to us or didn't happen for us. When I decided that everything happens for a reason and the reason is for me to learn, everything in my life became simpler and more manageable.

I simply decided that the answer to "why" was always for me to learn so I stopped asking it. And what stopped along with the question was the zillions of judgments that I would make about myself and others in an effort to answer that question.

When you stop looking for the reasons why good and bad things happen in life, you release tens of thousands of judgmental thoughts. These judgmental thoughts are just distractions from the lessons anyway. Judgment is rooted in fear and self-preservation and can keep you occupied for a lifetime. But that's not why you are here.

WARNING: Do not bypass all of your emotions because everything happens for a reason. Deciding to be positive instead of feeling your feelings is a dangerous practice that causes our unresolved emotions to compound in our bodies. This can create symptoms of anxiety, depression, panic, rage, migraines, hypertension, and more.

Let yourself feel your feelings and then when you're ready to move forward, look at what you have learned from the experience rather than trying to put it out of your mind.

About 15 years ago something difficult happened with my partner that was very painful and confusing. Telling you the story would tell his story too, so I'll save us all from that. But I'll tell you it was shocking, embarrassing, and painful.

My go-to question would be Why?! Why is this happening to me? Why me why not someone else? As I felt the emotions of this awful experience, I realized that I was noticing some positive things happening in my life from this situation. I no longer felt like a victim and actually felt like I was being set free.

I started to look at other times in my life when I had questioned why this is happening and looked at what I had learned or what had shifted as a result of the painful experience. I vowed to myself that I wasn't going to ask why anymore. Instead, I was going to choose the question, "What am I learning from this?"

Here are the questions that I ask myself instead:

What am I learning about the people involved?

What am I learning about myself?

What am I learning about how I think the world works?

Why would I have been a part of this learning?

These questions bring a sense of freedom into the situation and if you choose, you will feel empowered. You get to take responsibility and ownership of the circumstances of your life rather than feeling like you are just caught up in the waves of life with no choices and no power. Instead, asking these questions reminds you of your power of perspective and choice.

You can decide to ask why and get caught up in the waves or you can choose to feel all of your feelings. And then when it's time, ask yourself what you're learning so you can find your footing and discover your next steps.

I Learn From Everything.

affirmations

I trust that there's a lesson for me in every experience.

I trust that the Universe is constantly helping me grow.

Everything is happening for me rather than to me.

I release judgment of my experience and feel my feelings.

I allow my feelings to move through me rather than holding onto suffering.

I have faith in my ability to grow from every experience.

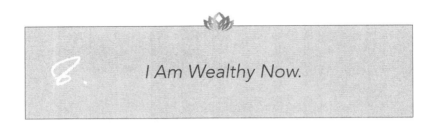

8.

I Am Wealthy Now.

*"Gratitude for the present moment and
the fullness of life now is the true prosperity."*
Eckhart Tolle

As a powerful creator and piece of the Divine, you are already wealthy.

You are connected to a constant, steady, limitless stream of love and abundance. Wealth is what you are from, so you must be wealth. You feeling any way other than wealthy and living a rich life is not serving anyone.

That guilty feeling that pops up when you see people struggling or having less than you, doesn't help them. That guilty feeling that makes you feel like you need to save or rescue them, doesn't help them. It keeps you from your bigger mission.

Yes, of course, you can feel loving and supportive and give generously as your heart desires. The guilt is actually coming from a place inside that is afraid of being better than someone else. Guess what? You're not better. They are not worse. You are on different journeys.

When you feel guilt about your success, that's about judging where other people are on their journeys. You can see how it is truly a distraction and not even something that comes from love. It comes from fear and ego trying to keep you small.

Release the judgment and free yourself to continue on your own journey so you can create the change in the world that you desire. Remember, your journey, big vision, and desires are yours for a reason. So there's no need to judge yourself or compare yourself to others.

The same is true when you see someone who you believe has more than you or is doing better than you. You're different people on different journeys. This time the fear is disguised as jealousy. Jealousy is about believing on some level that you can't have your desires because you're unworthy or undeserving or incapable for some reason. The fear and ego are trying to keep you small once again. Keeping you small helps you avoid change. The ego likes things just as they are. But you were meant for more.

You get to forgive yourself now for the times that you've felt this way in your life. You get to release yourself from judgment right now. You get to move forward into the new way of being that is more from love and less from fear.

You get to feel wealthy right now. Feel that wealth and abundance in all areas of your life, and tune in to what you are thinking and feeling in your body about money, wealth, abundance, connection, trust, love, joy, creativity, and fun and so on.

Think about your vision and your desire. Think about how it will feel when you are living that next level. Notice how it feels now that you've given yourself permission to commit to your desires. Notice how your body responds when you trust that you will always see what is meant for you.

A feeling of lack or scarcity can show up when you have no money (*obviously*) and other times when you worry about your responsibilities, the things you want, the places you want to go, the needs of your family, business, or community.

Often these responses and worries are happening when you are in chasing mode or feeling desperate rather than being open to receiving. Try not to judge yourself. Once again, simply acknowledge what is coming up for you rather than being frustrated with yourself.

Forgive the part of you that is scared, nervous, anxious, or desperate. Forgive yourself for creating those feelings. Forgive the path that has brought you here. That part of you simply feels very passionate about what you want. And there is a fear there of what will happen when you don't get it.

Put your hand on your heart and thank that part for being concerned. Use your own vocabulary and be very loving. Judging that part of yourself will just create more attachment to the feelings that are already uncomfortable. Validate the feelings that are coming up and help that part understand that you are creating opportunities for more wealth and abundance through your work, your business, and knowing and trusting that money can come to you from known and unknown sources at any time.

You may think of just pushing through or pushing past acknowledging your feelings and being loving with yourself. It might feel like a waste of time because you have big goals and visions. But you get to love yourself fiercely through this process. The part of you that feels fear needs to be acknowledged. If not, the fear will get louder.

The fear can be like when a child wants its mother's attention and it starts calling, "Mom! Mom!" And the mom is busy doing something else and doesn't answer right away, the child gets louder and louder. That's what happens to our fears when they are not validated or acknowledged. Except that unacknowledged fear getting louder and louder trying to get your attention shows itself as resentment, anxiety, panic, anger, rage, or depression.

You will never hear me coach you to shut down or ignore your feelings. Trying to ignore them will just create more noise in your thoughts and more discomfort. Comfort that part like you'd speak to a friend or loved one and then help it to see what you are already creating. Show it what connections you are creating in your life. Show it that you are taking action to make things better.

There will be times when money is needed urgently and the money isn't there and that can be terrifying. These are the moments when it is extremely important for you to acknowledge those feelings. This will help you free your mind, so you can get creative and inspired for opportunities to create some cash now. You receive more inspiration when your mind is calm than when you are fighting it to figure out what you are going to do.

Once you have acknowledged and forgiven yourself and feelings, it is time to shift your energy and expectation about what you have already created in your life so that you can bring that energy into your present state. You can do this simply and swiftly by practicing gratitude.

Gratitude saved my life. Maybe not my actual breathing and heartbeat, but it saved my sanity, my self-trust, and my worthiness.

I found gratitude during a time in my life when there was a lot of change and growth happening, and I was really in a place of finding my self-worth. There was something missing. I was giving and giving and giving and thought that would be enough.

I wasn't focused on all that was coming into my life. I wasn't celebrating the amazing life I was creating. Instead, I was focused on what I was still waiting for. I was focused on the stuff and people and experiences that I wanted. I was focused on the empty spaces.

What did I get from focusing on the places in my life that were lacking? I got sad, empty, wishing and longing, and lonely feelings. How did that serve me? Well it served my ego, didn't it? It was my ego saying, "nope, stay in lack and scarcity," even though my life was a lot better. Let's keep you from realizing your growth and changes. It kept me small and in worry … distracted from taking action toward my goals. Kept me feeling scarcity.

And I was good at scarcity already. As you know, I had been out of touch with my money. So it makes sense that I was dancing with scarcity. For example, I worried about paying my taxes so much that when I heard the tax preparers commercials on tv or radio, I would get a stomach ache.

I had so much going for me, but I was scared of this new unknown when my business was bringing in enough money to actually pay more taxes. I had buried my head in the sand and just let myself feel sick.

The same thing was happening again. This time it was about love. I had met someone very special but due to several circumstances, I had to make the decision to end it. We were so deeply connected after a few short weeks, but it wasn't going to work. When we parted, I felt intense lack and scarcity for the relationship that wasn't there anymore.

Sharing with my friend that maybe this was my last chance at love I was introduced to the book *The Magic* by Rhonda Byrne. As I write this, my current self, who is happily married to an amazing partner that I manifested, chuckles a bit at my lack of faith and also feels a deep love for this part of me that was so lost. (Don't worry about looking for it now. It's listed in the Recommended Reading.)

It started me on a path of noticing big and small moments of joy, celebration, deeply connecting to nature and sunrises, sunsets, my best friend's laugh, my mind, my creativity, my ideas, the carpet under my feet on a cold night, the special blanket that my grandmother made for me, the memories of the last conversations that I had with her before she passed away, the stories she told me about how she met my grandfather, how they fell in love, what his family went through to get here, and so on.

Often when I ask my clients to start practicing gratitude, they will tell me that their lists are pretty much the same every day. This is how I started too. My list would be that I'm thankful for my health, my home, my family, my job, my car, etc. This is a fine place to start, and you get to go deeper and wider into your gratitude because gratitude is how you celebrate life and how you feel wealthy right now and welcome in what is on its way to you.

Here's an example of how deeply this can go very quickly if you open up to it:

I love to read. I am very grateful for all the knowledge, understanding, and sparks of inspiration, and entertainment I get from reading. I am grateful that I can see the words and feel the book in my hands. I am grateful that I can comprehend what I am reading (most of the time). I am grateful that my mind has the ability to be stretched and will expand for new thoughts and ideas. I am grateful that my Mom would help me with my book reports when I was in third grade because I was a terrible procrastinator and would put off reading my book until the last day. She would read it and help me (okay more than help me) write a book report. I am grateful that when I informed her that I had a book report for Black Beauty due the next morning, it put her over the edge. She flat out refused to ever write another book report for me again.

THANK YOU, MOM!

I am grateful that the next book I chose was this yellow-covered book about a Chinese girl whose family owned a restaurant and they lived above it and that I loved that story about her and her family and her adventures so much that I fell in love with reading. I am so grateful that Mrs. Dorn taught our fifth-grade reading class to speed read, so I would love reading even more because it didn't take as long for me to read a book and I could now read so many more. I am grateful that I loved reading so much that it helped me tremendously through school and college. I am grateful that I wasn't afraid of big books with complicated theories because I trusted myself to be able to read and comprehend because I had been practicing since my yellow-covered book in 3rd grade.

I could go on.

Because I've practiced these streams of gratitude for over ten years now, I can find so much goodness in my everyday life. I can even find beauty in painful moments and lessons. And because of that, there is no limit to where I can find happiness and wealth in my life.

Here's a simple practice to get you started:

- Commit to writing ten things that you are grateful for every day.

- Write your gratitude statements answering these questions:

- What am I grateful for?

- Why am I grateful for it?

- How does it make me feel inside?

- When you've practiced this for a few days, let it expand by adding this question: What else is associated or attached to this experience that I can feel grateful for and then answer the first three questions again.

Physically put a pen to paper and write the words. Your brain processes things differently when you actually write them down. Create a notebook filled with all of the beauty of your life. Add quotes and song lyrics and illustrate words that you love.

Give yourself 5 days and then add 5 more and then try not to break the streak.

Do this before bed and your subconscious mind will cycle through these memories as you sleep. You'll sleep better. You'll wake up happier. As you continue your practice you'll unlock your ability to see mountains of abundance in your own life.

In case you need an extra bonus you'll slow down and eventually stop comparing your life to everyone else's because you'll be so happy with your own.

I Am Wealthy Now.

affirmations

As I look around my life I have everything that I need right now.

I give myself permission to feel wealthy now.

I allow myself to feel joy at my abundance now.

I see wealth pouring into my life every single day.

I enjoy celebrating everything in my life as a form of abundance.

I am wealthy now.

9. I Honor My Power of Choice.

"Big things are built one brick at a time.
Victories are achieved one choice at a time.
A life well-lived is chosen one day at a time."
Lysa TerKeurst

Each and every day as you are committed to your desires, you choose actions, steps, thoughts, beliefs, and feelings to get you there. You decide how long it will take based on how much effort and energy you put into it.

You decide how happy you allow yourself to be based on what you allow yourself to think, feel, and how you allow yourself to behave.

You make decisions all day every day moving toward your vision or further away.

You make thousands of decisions every day and most of them turn out just fine without any upset, drama, or even another thought. You decide when to wake up, get out of bed, if you brush your teeth, what to wear, what to eat, how to care for yourself, how to care for your children, when to go to do your work, when to stop, who to talk to, who to avoid, when to protect yourself, when to go for it, and so on. You make millions upon millions of choices over a lifetime.

Each and every one of those millions of choices gives you control. You are either moving closer to, away from, or in alignment with your desires and visions for your life.

How you choose to think.

How you choose to behave.

What words you choose.

What ideas you spread.

What energy you share.

What information you consume.

Which tea bags you like.

Who you spend your time with.

What stories you tell.

What pictures you print and which ones you delete.

What love you give.

What forgiveness you offer.

What healing you find.

What you teach your children.

Who you judge.

Who you support.

This list goes on and on.

Every choice you make tells a story of how connected you are to your vision, mission, and purpose.

This isn't a reminder to be perfect.

PLEASE DO NOT TRY FOR PERFECTION!

This is a reminder about just how powerful you are.

Imagine practicing making decisions from an intention about living a rich, fulfilling life of love, connection, trust, faith, joy or whatever life you want to create.

You get to dive deeply into what feels the very best for you. There is no one else who can make those choices for you because they don't know your heart. They don't know your vision. Asking someone for advice in this area will stir up their own fear and give you an opportunity to release responsibility of your success, progress, and happiness to someone else.

Start paying attention to what you really want and then build your decisions from there. As you make decisions in alignment with your vision, you will inevitably choose to leave circumstances, relationships, jobs, limiting beliefs, and more behind.

You are allowed without self-judgment to walk away from things that no longer serve you. You don't have to worry about how much time you've put into something or how much money you will lose. If it no longer feels right, good, or natural to you and you're honest with yourself about whether or not your decision is from fear or from clarity, you get to walk away without second-guessing yourself.

You can decide to make a decision and choose to take the action at some date in the future. You get to change your mind as your heart guides you.

Choices create shifts. Shifts create change. Change creates change. As you make intentional choices, the things in your life will start to look differently because you will see them in a different light. This is good. This reminds you that when you put your heart into your life with your power of choice, things will move.

Dr. Wayne Dyer's words come to mind now: "When I change the way that I look at things, the things I look at change."

As you grow and change you will become more yourself than ever. Some things will become more important to you while other things will naturally fade away.

When healing is more important, holding grudges will be less important. Creating a fulfilling life will be more important than comparing yourself to others. Having a loyal circle of friends will be more important than having hundreds of friends. Having wonderful clients will become more important than thousands of social media followers. Living and holding space for a lasting love with a trusting partner will feel more freeing than holding onto the wrong partner. When your mission is more important to you, what people think of you and your ideas will be less important.

Knowing your life the way that you do, think about making meaningful choices with intention. Imagine what is possible for you.

Your choices are your activism. Your choices influence your world and your experiences. Your choices influence the people around you and their experiences. You are modeling behaviors to your loved ones and people you have never met with your choices.

My sister once told me that her life and her childrens' lives are exponentially better because of the path I have chosen for my life. The things I've learned, the experiences I've had, the lessons that I have shared impact the way that they think and respond every day. My dear friend told me recently, "I'm so thankful for you! I don't know what I would do without you! My life would be completely different if I hadn't met you."

Please remember that you are rippling out energy and influence with every choice that you make.

You can choose to put this book down, deciding that you've read and understood it well enough that you don't have to hang onto it. You can decide the standards are so simple they can't possibly be enough to change your life. You can decide that it's all common sense because you may have heard something like them before.

OR...

You can take hold of each standard and create a really special life for yourself.

You can let your growth into a wealthy woman be as simple and uncomplicated as I've shared it with you.

You can choose to share it with your friends and decide to keep it as a reminder that you can create your desires.

You can ask your friends to join you in creating lives filled with intention and fulfillment.

You can make agreements with one another to practice together being the best version of yourselves that you can be.

Whatever you choose to do, something will shift in your life. You will be moving in a slightly different direction.

I encourage you to remember that whatever you choose shifts things, so make your decisions from love and alignment with your desires.

9. I Honor My Power of Choice.

affirmations

I trust in my ability to make good choices.

I choose with intention rather than settle.

I trust myself and my vision with meaningful choices.

I get to choose what I see for myself.

I trust myself to change as my heart guides me.

I get to choose and choose again.

I honor my ability to decide what is within my
standards and what is outside of my standards.

I Operate From Love.

"The more you are motivated by love, the more fearless and free your actions will be."
Dalai Lama

Every single one of our feelings, emotions, and responses is rooted in fear or in love. Some of the fears might be that we aren't going to be okay, we aren't going to be safe, we aren't going to be loved, we aren't going to be accepted, we aren't going to succeed, or that we aren't good enough in some way.

Our fears can show up as jealousy, anger, rage, panic, anxiety, frustration, self-sabotage, irritation, overwhelm, indifference, disconnection, mistrust, confusion, dishonesty, and more. A clue to know if you are feeling a fear-based feeling is that it will likely feel tense, heavy, tight, hot, pressure, stomach churning, head pressure, or feeling generally yucky.

Emotions like faith, trust, love, passion, enthusiasm, positive expectation, optimism, hopefulness, gratitude, and even contentment are rooted in love. Love shows itself in these instances as self-worth, self-esteem, self-trust, and what comes from these feelings is confidence.

Confidence is not fearlessness of everything, but rather the trust in yourself to feel the whole spectrum of emotions and still be okay. Confidence is being willing to take calculated risks in your life in the direction of your desires that may lead to being rejected, being imperfect, losing, making mistakes, being embarrassed, being exposed, getting your feelings hurt, and in some cases risking injury like in skydiving or trying a new sport for the sake of your dreams, goals, and vision.

Confidence has at its core a self-trust that says, whatever you try, even if it's uncomfortable, I'm willing to take the step and do it because it's the next step to the goal. Confidence says I'm willing to try even if the outcome isn't great because I trust in my vision. Confidence says there is something greater here, and in order to see it, I have to try something I've never tried before.

Confidence is a practice, and it's a muscle. Don't expect it to be perfect and then judge yourself for not feeling it like your favorite superhero. Keep loving yourself, and when in doubt, love yourself some more.

Love is the place that you can respond and act from with minimal regret. Regret is a waste of time because it distracts from the present moment and puts us back in the past. It causes all sorts of judgment and replaying, rehashing the past but doesn't actually fix anything.

When you operate from love, your creative channels are open, your heart is open, you are using acknowledgement rather than judgment, you choose your actions based on your values and standards rather than your fears, and you are in the present moment with the future in mind. When you operate from love, regrets are few and far between.

Operating from fear looks like harsh judgments, gossiping, jealousy, comparison, being unkind, name calling, blaming, shaming, lying, cheating, stealing, hurting yourself or someone else (physically, emotionally, or otherwise), ignoring, neglecting, avoiding, running away, giving the silent treatment, diving inward into deep analysis, self sabotage, and so on.

When you feel yourself wanting to step into any of these or other behaviors that cause you regrets, pause, take a moment, tune into your body, your mind, and notice what is happening inside. There's a lot of power in that pause. You can change your whole life by pausing and paying attention to what's happening inside of you before you act or react. This is your moment to decide what happens next.

You can continue on the path and behave as you were going to, or you can take a breath, acknowledge and validate your feelings, and then move yourself over to love and operate from there.

Even as you read that it feels more open. You can breathe deeper, you can think more clearly, and you can assess the consequences of your next actions.

Since you want more for yourself than what you've given yourself in the past, you can easily step into this practice. It'll create more ease in your life. You'll get to have more joy, more fun, more gratitude, more creativity, and more of everything good.

Operating from love and letting that be the foundation of your life and actions will not make your life perfect. Bad things will still happen, and there will still be pain because life is up and down and twisting and turning in it's beautiful messiness. No matter how messy it gets, the percentage of time that you get to pause and choose your feelings, emotions, thinking, and behavior remain at 100%.

No matter what has happened, you get to operate from love (dig deep if you have to) and choose your next steps. Whether that is more love, change of habits, more visibility, starting that business, expanding your business, making your annual income your monthly income, finding a coach or hypnotist, changing your relationship status, moving out, or starting over, you have everything inside of you to do it.

I promise you that you can do the hard things. You can make the changes. You can heal your mind. You can be brave. You can choose more for yourself even with your current circumstances. You can move your life in a whole new direction one degree, one decision, one loving breath at a time.

10.   *I Operate From Love.*

affirmations

When my choices are love or fear, I choose love every time.

As I let my heart guide me, I operate from love.

Even though I am imperfect, I deeply and completely love and accept myself.

Love is the language of my heart.

I find my way back to love and choose from there.

PART THREE

living your rich life

WHAT COMES NEXT

*"Live with intention. Walk to the edge.
Listen hard. Practice wellness. Play with abandon.
Laugh. Choose with no regret. Do what you love.
Live as if this is all there is."*
Mary Anne Roadacher-Hershey

What is next for you?

Everything.

That's what's next for you. You get to decide what it is that you really want and create it for yourself.

Take some time to complete this special "vision test" and let yourself get really clear on what you desire for yourself.

Rules:
There are no rules.

Let your vision go wild.

Unleash your imagination.

There are no wrong answers.

Write it even if it doesn't make any sense to you now.

Give yourself at least 15 minutes and take as long as you want.

Once you begin writing, you may have a rush of items that you've had in your mind already. The speed might slow down a bit after you've written your top ten things.

Place your hand on your heart and breath. Drop down into this loving place inside of you that guides you and loves you simultaneously. Allow the flow to continue from your heart and what matters most to you. Do not judge what comes out of your pen. Let it flow. You can refine and find timelines later. Release yourself from the worry of how you'll make this happen.

Organize them into these sections:
Health and Fitness
Fun and Experiences
Spiritual and Personal Development
Family and Relationships
Business/Career and Finance
Legacy and Contribution

Prioritize which are most important. Your heart will call out to which ones are urgent. Your ego may have you put the more difficult ideas a lower priority. Do not judge the ego for doing that. Simply give it the love that it needs, acknowledge the fears, and then with gentle firmness help it see the vision. Create the pictures in your mind with you in them acting out your vision, your dreams, you accomplishments.

This is a reminder to keep communicating with these parts of you. Each part of you has the power of influence. It's important to stay connected to what you really want, so your mind gets used to thinking about it, feeling what it will feel like, and having a crystal clear picture of it just like the builder who keeps the house plans close at hand for constant reference.

Through practicing living these standards, you get to see your life and everything in it through different eyes. The eyes of possibility, potential, and freedom. No longer will the unknown be a place of fear, it will be a place of limitless possibilities. You get to enjoy the simple things with greater joy.

When you begin to live by the standards and you choose this way of being each and every day, the world opens up for you. When you get really clear on your vision and live this way, you will start taking actions in alignment with that vision.

Your vision will unfold for you with each and every breath, action, feeling, and behavior. You will notice your ability to shift your circumstances by shifting your feelings, thoughts, and behaviors.

So what do you really want?

Start with what you think you can get and then go deeper.

What do you really, really want?

What are those secret thoughts in your head?

What is that quiet vision that you've never really shared with anyone?

Imagine yourself with those dreams fulfilled and then let yourself go further.

If you had all of your current desires what would you want next?

Your journey and path is to fully embody this free, wealthy, loving, confident, worthy, wealthy woman version of yourself.

You get to practice being this perfectly imperfect version of yourself to live a life of your design and desire. Practicing is about taking imperfect action in alignment with your goals, visions, and desires.

Write down your next action steps even if they seem tiny to you. Break the bigger steps into smaller ones.

Write down what you need to support you getting there.

You are a powerful, wealthy woman operating from love. You are responsible for your energy, happiness, and success. You are committed to your desires. You always see what is meant for you. You learn from everything. And you always honor your power of choice.

What steps come next?

Who helps you?

Who supports you?

What resources will you need?

Create your action plan. It doesn't have to be fancy. Just write down the steps that you know and leave room for the steps you'll discover.

Do not let this activity be the last action you take toward your vision today. Ride the wave of this energy and make a declaration, tell a friend, make a decision, set a date, ask for support, take another step in the direction of your vision right now. You deserve it.

Everything will open up for you as you take loving action from your Wealthy Woman Standards.

I believe in you.

Love, *Rebecca*

ACKNOWLEDGMENTS

To God, Universe, and Divine Source of All, thank you for placing this passion in my heart and constantly reminding me why I chose this path.

To Joel, my Angel and magic man, thank you for support, encouragement, and always reminding me to expect miracles. I love living in abundance with you.

To Makenzie, my daughter, thank you for showing me the world through your compassionate eyes.

To Mom, Dad, Elli, and Jonathan, and the family we've created, I am constantly grateful for the humor and Kodak® moments we share. I couldn't have chosen a better family. Our shared experiences sent me on this journey to help and heal the world, and I am grateful for this path every single day.

To Donnette and the McGregors, Your love and support took my life to another level. Thank you.

To Ally, thank you for that moment so long ago as we sat across the table from one another. I'll never forget that moment of sisterhood.

To Jess, thank you for your trust, commitment, and for holding us together while reminding me that women need this message.

To Nana, thank you for helping me find my words. "The most."

To Stephanie, thank you for unwavering sisterhood.

To My Besties + Moon Sisters, never in a million years did I think I would be so blessed with such magical sisters who would reveal themselves as my soul mates. Thank you so much for celebrating every step of this journey with me. I am grateful for getting to share this life with you. Let's meet one another sooner next time.

My Shandara Sisters, thank you for believing and holding the vision with me. I feel your love in the golden spiral callback.

To Johnny, I know you're with me every step. "Take it easy."

To My Aunties, I feel your faith in me, always.

To my teachers and coaches who have poured love into me, thank you for opening my eyes to my blind spots and lovingly guiding my transformation.

To Jordan, thank you for your special part in my journey.

To 27 and Lionheart, thank you for helping me stretch.

To FA, BOD, R&R, BPW, and BNI, thank you for your part in helping me learn to speak confidently about my work and create success in my life and business.

To My Entrepreneur Friends, I see you and I thank you for making the world better with your love and passion.

To my past, present, and future clients, thank you for teaching me new perspectives and helping me learn that trust is my love language.

To you, the reader, thank you for choosing to be here. This is my love letter to you.

It is with great joy that I acknowledge if I listed every person who added to my life in a special way, this list would be longer than the entirety of this book.

CONNECT WITH REBECCA

Rebecca Wiener McGregor is an Amplifier of Love and catalyst for breakthroughs! She shares her gifts as a transformational hypnotist + money mindset coach committed to helping visionary women live their Truth, step into their Divine Purpose, and create the life of their dreams. Since 2004, she has helped thousands of clients to release old blocks, physical, emotional, and sexual traumas, loss, and hidden fears to find a deeper sense of self-worth and determination to live life on their own terms. Using that self-worth and determination as fuel to create the life they've been dreaming of with deeper connection, more joy, more impact, wealth, and more fun!

Rebecca's clients include spiritual entrepreneurs, coaches, healers, executives, entertainers, and influencers—women who have a message to share with the world. She's worked with women across the country and around the world to release limiting beliefs and rewire their subconscious minds to feel limitless, take action, and create a life filled with abundance. Rebecca lives with her husband (in a relationship she manifested) and her rescue dogs Lucy, Millie, and Winston in South Dakota, USA where she loves watching the water, books, art, music, has the ever-so-slight Netflix infatuation, and loves spending time hosting her friends and family.

If you are ready to do the deep healing so that you can trust yourself to be in alignment with and embody these standards and to create the life you want, I can guide you to stop recreating anxiety, fear, sadness, depression, rage, or stuckness. Reach out for a consultation at **www.rebeccawiener.com/schedule/** to work with me privately. I'll walk the path with you to create healing, forgiveness, acceptance, confidence, and fulfillment.

If you are ready to rewire your mind to create wealth and abundance in every area of your life join Extraordinary Wealth Course + Community here: **www.ewrightnow.com**

Join my FREE online community: **InnerCircleWithRebecca.com**

Websites:
RebeccaWiener.com
HealWithHypnosis.com

Social Media:
https://www.facebook.com/iamrebeccasue
https://www.linkedin.com/in/iamrebeccasue/
https://www.instagram.com/iamrebeccasue/

QR CODE LINKS

RebeccaWiener.com

HealWithHypnosis.com

My Podcast

ewrightnow.com

RECOMMENDED READING

Untethered Soul by Michael A Singer

The Four Agreements by Don Miguel Ruiz

The Magic by Rhonda Byrne

Zero Limits by Joe Vitale

The Power of your Subconscious Mind by Joseph Murphy

The Power of Intention by Dr Wayne Dyer

Outrageous Openness by Tosha Silver

Change Me Prayers by Tosha Silver

The Artist's Way by Julia Cameron

Answered Prayers: Love Letters from the Divine
by Julia Cameron

Manifesting Miracles by Neville Goddard

The New Revelations: A Conversation With God
by Neale Donald Walsch

The Power Of Now: A Guide to Spiritual Enlightenment
by Eckhart Tolle

Live With Intention by Mary Anne Roadacher-Hershey

*The Book of Awakening: Having the Life You Want by Being
Present to the Life You Have* by Mark Nepo

Ask and It Is Given: Learning to Manifest Your Desires
by Esther Hicks , Jerry Hicks , et al.

CITATIONS

Study quoted on page 12:
Osili, U., Clark, C., Bergdoll, J., Ehrenfeld, J., Costello, C., Fitzgerald, J., Howell, G., Galligan, K., Jarvis, W., Porzio, D., & Slugg, R. (2018, October 24). *IUPUI*. The 2018 U.S. Trust® Study of High Net Worth Philanthropy. Retrieved December 6, 2021, from https://scholarworks.iupui.edu/handle/1805/17667.

Printed in Great Britain
by Amazon